# Plyometrics

*Complete Training for all Sports*

## by
## Will and Evelyn Freeman

CHAMPIONSHIP BOOKS
P.O. Box 1166, ISU Station
Ames, Iowa 50010

© Copyright 1984 by Championship Books, Ames, Iowa.
ISBN 0-89279-068-7
All rights reserved. No part of this book may be reproduced in any form or by any means without permission in writing from the publisher.

# About the Authors

Will and Evelyn Freeman are the track and field coaches at Grinnell (Iowa) College. Both are former track and field athletes. At the University of Florida, Will won All-America honors and 3 indoor and 2 outdoor Southeastern Conference titles in the pole vault. With a best performance of 17' 8", he competed at both the 1976 and 1980 U.S. Olympic Trials and represented the U.S. in international competition. Evelyn was one of the top high jumpers in Canada and competed at the 1972 and 1976 Canadian Olympic Trials. With a best height of 6', she finished 2nd at the Canadian National Championships. Evelyn and Will are accomplished athletes in several sports other than track and field, and Will teaches biomechanics and serves as chairman of the physical education department at Grinnell.

Will holds a bachelor's degree from Florida and a master's degree from Indiana University, while Evelyn has bachelor's degrees from York University (Toronto) and the University of Toronto.

# Preface

Our travels as track and field athletes have exposed us to many different types of training philosophies and techniques. This book is devoted to one of those techniques — Plyometrics. We hope this work will shed light on a subject that is relatively new to the U.S. athletic scene. Plyometrics are adaptable to sports such as track and field, football, baseball, and basketball that utilize quick powerful movements. Proper use of these techniques can add to the speed, quickness, and jumping and throwing abilities of athletes. We have successfully used these techniques for several years with our track teams at Grinnell College.

We are greatly indebted to Andy Higgins and Zolten Tenke, track coaches at the University of Toronto. As the Canadian national multi-events and longjump coordinators, these two men first exposed us to the positive effects of Plyometrics when we were training in Toronto. Thanks also go to Bill Bergan of Iowa State University who was instrumental in the publishing of this work. Finally, thanks to Rich Gilbreaith and Doug Bailey of Grinnell for their assistance in the filming of the drills.

Will and Evelyn Freeman

# Foreword

Too often, a new training system appears on the sporting scene and creates more confusion and misunderstanding than was ever intended. Such has been the case with plyometric training, or plyometrics. Plyometrics have been around for almost two decades, yet few American coaches and athletes have taken full advantage of their benefits.

*Plyometrics: Complete Training for All Sports,* by Will and Evelyn Freeman, fills the void between the scientist and the coach. Used without complete understanding, plyometric training can be more destructive than helpful in the development of champion athletes. Under proper guidance, plyometrics can be one of the most effective means of achieving athletic success. The Freemans have provided a vehicle for gaining improved sport performance.

Both Will and Evelyn were athletes who competed on the international level. Throughout their book, this exceptional talent is evident as their trained eyes and minds reveal the small, unnoticed tips that give coaches and athletes the added boost toward better productivity.

*Plyometrics: Complete Training for All Sports* is a breakthrough publication that will eventually take its rightful place among other pioneering efforts in the literary world of athletics. Emphasis throughout the book has concentrated on the practical by the generous use of photographs and drill descriptions.

Coaches at any level of competition will find this book on plyometrics to be understandable and useful for any sport.

Bill Bergan
Track Coach
Iowa State University

# Table of Contents

I. **INTRODUCTION** .......................... 1
   History .......................................... 1
   Description ...................................... 1
II. **THE PHYSIOLOGY OF THE PLYOMETRIC CONCEPT** ................... 2
   The Stretch Reflex ............................. 2
   The Storage of Elastic Energy .................... 2
III. **WHEN SHOULD PLYOMETRICS BE IMPLEMENTED?** ....................... 4
   Surfaces for Plyometric Training .................. 5
IV. **WHAT IS HOPPING AND BOUNDING?** ........ 6
   Basic Hopping and Bounding Drills ................ 6
   Picture Descriptions of Hopping and Bounding ...... 9
V. **WHAT IS DEPTH JUMPING?** ............... 26
   Basic Depth Jumping Drills ..................... 27
   Picture Descriptions of Depth Jumping ............ 29
VI. **PLYOMETRIC THROWING DRILLS** ......... 33
   Picture Descriptions of Throwing Drills ............ 35
VII. **COACHING POINTS** ..................... 42
VIII. **SUGGESTED PLYOMETRIC ROUTINES** ..... 44
   Early Pre-season ............................... 44
   Pre-Season ..................................... 44
   Competitive Season ............................ 45
   **REFERENCES** .......................... 46

x

# Chapter I

**INTRODUCTION**

Plyometrics though relatively new in North America, are a training technique which have been used extensively in the Soviet Union and throughout Eastern European countries since the early 1960's. Plyometric exercises are used to improve maximal strength and speed of movement which result in an increase of explosive power. Dynamic in nature, these drills satisfy the basic training principle of specificity, practice with movements similar in nature and speed to the skill or event for which one is training. Because it simulates quick movements better than most weight lifting exercises, this training method should be supplemental to a weight training program.

**HISTORY**

Early research on plyometrics focused mainly on depth jumping exercises with little interest in hopping and bounding drills. Verhoshanski is accredited with advancing public thought on the subject through a 1966 article on speed-strength development of Soviet jumpers. Most research on the subject in the 1960's and 1970's was done in the Soviet Union and Eastern European countries.

Herman Parcells and others began to study the subject in the United States during the mid 1970's. The effects of plyometrics were substantiated with the performances of Valery Borzov, 1972 Olympic 100M and 200M Champion and Pat Matzdorf, former World Record Holder, high jump.

**DESCRIPTION**

The term plyometrics can be used to include both depth jumping and hopping and bounding drills. They are very dynamic movements which use gravitational force on the body and the contractibility and elasticity of muscle tissue to increase the force or stress on related muscles.

# Chapter II

**THE PHYSIOLOGY OF THE PLYOMETRIC CONCEPT**
The basic concept of plyometric exercises involves the stretch reflex mechanism and the storage of elastic energy.

**THE STRETCH REFLEX**
As an athlete lands on the ground during a plyometric exercise, a stretch occurs in the involved muscle fibers. Proprioceptors within the muscle tissues immediately sense this stretch and send a message to the spinal cord through an afferent, or sensory neuron. The spinal cord sends an immediate message back to the muscle fiber via an efferent, or motor neuron, telling it to contract to keep it from overstretching. This is known as the "stretch reflex" and it is one of the body's built-in protection mechanisms for prevention of injuries to muscle tissues. Plyometric drills can be used to train the body to emit these sensor signals in a shorter time period which cause the affected muscle to react more quickly.

The action of plyometric jumping involves an initial eccentric contraction, or stretching of the muscle upon landing, followed *immediately* by a concentric contraction, or shortening of the muscle during the take-off. This means that the athlete falls back to the ground from a previous jump, absorbs the gravitational force on his body during the stretch of eccentric contraction and immediately returns to the jump phase by initiating a concentric contraction.

**THE STORAGE OF ELASTIC ENERGY**
Hochmuth (1974) stated that, "A body movement, requiring an extremely high end velocity can best be achieved by starting it with a movement in the opposite direction. The braking of the opposite movement . . . creates positive acceleration power for the original movement."

For example, as a batter swings at a ball he first moves the bat in the reverse direction of the forward swing. This backward movement, or "hitch," and subsequent forward movement puts a "stretch" on the involved muscle groups. This stretch stores kinetic energy in the muscle and creates a greater concentric contraction as the bat is swung forward. The pre-stretch is often referred to as "loading a muscle."

During the eccentric phase of the plyometric jumping movement, the muscles are actively loading kinetic energy even while being forcibly stretched. The kinetic energy is immediately released during the subsequent concentric contraction or rebound. In short, a jump will be higher if preceded by another jump because the energy stored by the muscles during the falling (stretch) phase of the first jump will be released during the subsequent concentric (shortening) muscle contraction.

An important consideration is the speed at which the eccentric contraction is followed by the concentric contraction. The faster the muscles are forced to lengthen, the greater the stress upon the involved muscles and subsequently the greater the rebounding concentric contraction will be. When performing these plyometric drills, emphasis should be placed upon keeping the "lag" time between contact and rebound as short as possible.

# Chapter III

**WHEN SHOULD PLYOMETRICS BE IMPLEMENTED?**

As previously stated, plyometric drills place a great deal of stress upon the body. To ensure that your athletes are able to adapt to this type of training without injury, a weight lifting program should be used before plyometrics are started. Training with weights should develop the necessary strength needed to perform plyometric exercises safely. However, plyometrics should *not* replace a weight training program. Supplement plyometrics with both a strength program and a running program. Power includes both the elements of speed and strength and *plyometrics help to integrate the two.*

A basic weight training program for over-all conditioning should include the following exercises:

| | |
|---|---|
| Sit-ups | 3 sets of 30 repetitions |
| Split Squats | 3 sets of 10 repetitions |
| Half Squats | 3 sets of 10 repetitions |
| Power Cleans | 3 sets of 10 repetitions |
| Bench Press | 3 sets of 10 repetitions |
| Hamstring Curls | 3 sets of 10 repetitions |
| Heel Raises | 3 sets of 10 repetitions |
| Step-ups | 3 sets of 10 repetitions |

All exercises should emphasize speed of movement and full range of motion. Because the above program is a general conditioning program, skills such as the throwing events in track and field warrant a slightly different program.

The intensity of the plyometric program should be dependent upon two factors:

**1. The athlete's age and physical capabilities**

One of the positive aspects of plyometric training is that the athlete tends to do the proper amount of work for his/her own physical structure. A stronger, more physically mature athlete can usually jump higher than a weaker, or younger athlete. By jumping higher, the stronger athlete enhances the gravitational acceleration and increases the resulting contraction off the ground. A weaker athlete is not likely to jump as high and will not subject his/her body to the stresses that a stronger athlete can handle.

**2. The time of year—pre-season, early competitive season, late competitive season.**

The time of year has a direct bearing on the amount of work the athlete should do. Gradually introduce your athletes to hopping and bounding during the pre-season. Limit the exercises to a few of the easier drills for the first one or two weeks and repeat the sets only once or twice.

As strength is gained and joints adapt to the stress, more difficult drills can be added and the number of repetitions can be increased. Depth jumping exercises from boxes should not be introduced until the athletes have mastered the hopping and bounding exercises and are strong enough to handle the additional stress.

The authors recommend that plyometrics be done one to two times each week during the pre-season and early competitive season; one time per week during the late competitive season; and not at all approximately two weeks prior to the main target competition.

It is also recommended that workouts be scheduled so that the plyometric routines are done on non-weight lifting days and at the end of the workout when the muscles, ligaments, and tendons are sufficiently warmed up and stretched out. Because plyometrics place a great deal of stress on the body, it is critical that athletes have at least a 48 hour recovery period between plyometric workouts. Coaches should constantly monitor their athletes to make sure that they are getting enough rest from the combination of plyometric and weight training.

**SURFACES FOR PLYOMETRIC TRAINING**

NEVER perform plyometric exercises on a hard surface such as a track, asphalt, or a basketball floor. If the surface does not "give," the possibility of shin splints, knee, and back injuries is increased. Use of gymnastic or wrestling mats is recommended for indoor training and a smooth stretch of soft grass is advisable outdoors.

It is suggested that each set of exercises covers a distance of between 20 and 40 meters depending upon the time of year and the fitness level of the athletes.

# Chapter IV

**WHAT IS HOPPING AND BOUNDING?**
Hopping and bounding drills are a series of jumping exercises which stress the joint areas of the ankles, knees, and hips to varying degrees depending upon the particular jumping drill.
Hopping can be done by jumping from *one* foot and landing on the *same* foot or by taking off and landing on both feet.
Bounding drills alternate from *one* foot to the *opposite* foot.
For variation, hopping can also be combined with bounding.
Emphasis can also be placed on jumping for height, distance, or both height and distance.

**BASIC HOPPING AND BOUNDING DRILLS**
(Explanation of techniques accompany pictures)
**Pre-Hopping and Bounding Drills** (warm-up)
  high knee running
  butt kick running
  4 X 4 (alternate 4 high knee, 4 butt kick)
  majorette stepping
  1 leg easy hopping*

**Two-Legged Hopping Drills**
  2 legged hopping—knees straight, for height
  2 legged hopping—knees straight, for distance
  2 legged hopping—knees to chest, for height
  2 legged hopping—heels to butt, for height
  2 legged squat jumps, for height
  2 legged squat jumps, for distance

**One-Legged Hopping Drills***
  1 legged hopping—knees straight, for height
  1 legged hopping for height & distance
  1 legged hopping for speed

*When performing a 1-legged exercise, always repeat the exercise with the opposite leg.

**Bounding Drills**
  high knee skipping, for height
  high knee skipping, for distance
  alternate bounding—knees straight, for height
  alternate bounding, for height
  alternate bounding, for distance
  alternate bounding, for height & distance
  repeat triple jumps, for height & distance
  fast feet running
  lunge jumps

**Variations**
2 legged hopping, with a twist
2 legged star jumps, for height
2 legged Czar jumps, for height
2 legged jump spins, with 90° turns
alternate double hops, (hop, step, hop, step)
2 legged squat jumps with medicine ball, for height
2 legged hopping over hurdles

Note: For added stress, a few of these drills can be done up a slight incline or up stairs. Examples are one-legged hopping, alternate bounding, two-legged squat jumps.

# Hopping and Bounding Drills

## Picture Descriptions

## HIGH KNEE RUNNING

**Coaching Points:** Emphasize high knee action and aggressive arm action.

## BUTT KICK RUNNING

**Coaching Points:** Emphasize aggressive arm action. As heels kick buttocks, knee should be directly under hip joint.

## 4 X 4

**Coaching Points:** Emphasize a full range of motion for both movements.
Alternate four high knee and four butt kicks.

## MAJORETTE STEPPING

**Coaching Points:** Drive knee as high as possible, then kick foot out.
There is a small skip step between each majorette step.
This is a great drill for hurdlers.

## ONE LEG EASY HOPPING

**Coaching Points:** This is an easy warm-up drill, do not emphasize the height or distance of each hop. Repeat with opposite leg.

## TWO LEGGED HOPPING—KNEES STRAIGHT, FOR HEIGHT

**Coaching Points:** Minimal flexion in the knee joint to isolate muscles in the calf.
Drive the arms aggressively upward.

**TWO LEGGED HOPPING—KNEES STRAIGHT, FOR DISTANCE**

**Coaching Points:** Minimal knee flexion, isolate calf muscles. Drive the arms aggressively forward.

**TWO LEGGED HOPPING—KNEES TO CHEST, FOR HEIGHT**

**Coaching Points:** Keep the upper body vertical—bring the knees to the chest, not the chest to the knees. Drive aggressively with the arms.

## TWO LEGGED HOPPING—HEELS TO BUTT, FOR HEIGHT

**Coaching Points:** Keep the upper body vertical. Drive arms up aggressively.

## TWO LEGGED SQUAT JUMPS FOR HEIGHT

**Coaching Points:** Knees should flex at a 90° angle during squat. Keep upper body as vertical as possible. Drive arms up aggressively and *block* with arms at chest level.

## TWO LEGGED SQUAT JUMPS FOR DISTANCE

**Coaching Points:** These are repetitive standing long jumps. There is *no pause* upon landing, immediately initiate the next jump.
Drive the arms forward.


## ONE LEGGED HOPPING—KNEES STRAIGHT FOR HEIGHT

**Coaching Points:** Minimal flexion at the knee joint.

## ONE LEGGED HOPPING FOR HEIGHT AND DISTANCE

**Coaching Points:** Use the free leg as a pendulum. As the takeoff leg moves forward during flight the free leg swings back to counterbalance. As the takeoff leg moves forward, foot kicks butt and lead knee drives forward and up. Initiate this exercise from a jogging start.

## ONE LEGGED HOPPING FOR SPEED

**Coaching Points:** Emphasize the turnover rate. Initiate from a jogging start.

## HIGH KNEE SKIPPING FOR HEIGHT

**Coaching Points:** Drive the lead knee and arms up aggressively.

## HIGH KNEE SKIPPING FOR DISTANCE

**Coaching Points:** Drive the lead knee and arms aggressively forward and up.

## ALTERNATE BOUNDING—KNEES STRAIGHT

**Coaching Points:** Minimal knee flexion.

## ALTERNATE BOUNDING FOR HEIGHT

**Coaching Points:** Drive lead knee and arms aggressively forward and up.

## ALTERNATE BOUNDING FOR DISTANCE

**Coaching Points:** Keep the center of gravity as level as possible.
Drive lead knee and arms aggressively forward and up.
Initiate from a jogging start.

## ALTERNATE BOUNDING FOR HEIGHT AND DISTANCE

**Coaching Points:** Drive lead knee and arms aggressively forward and up.
Initiate from a jogging start.

## REPEAT TRIPLE JUMPS FOR HEIGHT AND DISTANCE

**Coaching Points:** Initiate from a jogging start.
Keep distance of each hop, step, and jump as even as possible.
Use double arm action and drive forward and upward.

## FAST FEET RUNNING

**Coaching Points:** Emphasize turnover rate.
Coordinate arm action with leg action.

## LUNGE JUMPS

**Coaching Points:** Keep upper body vertical.
Emphasize long stride.
No pause between lunges.

## TWO LEGGED HOPPING WITH TWIST

**Coaching Points:** Use a recovery hop between each twisting motion.
Look over shoulder to feet, driving arms forward to act as a counterbalance.

## TWO LEGGED STAR JUMPS FOR HEIGHT

**Coaching Points:** Start from a squat position with knees flexed at 90°.

## TWO LEGGED CZAR JUMPS FOR HEIGHT

**Coaching Points:** Emphasize the quickness of each jump.

## TWO LEGGED JUMP SPINS WITH 90° TURNS

**Coaching Points:** Make two 90° hopping turns in same direction, then change direction and make two 90° hopping turns in the opposite direction.
Keep repeating as the athlete moves down the floor.

## ALTERNATE DOUBLE HOPS FOR HEIGHT AND DISTANCE

**Coaching Points:** Drive the lead knee and arms aggressively forward and up.
Initiate from a jogging start.
Hop, step, hop, step.

## TWO LEGGED SQUAT JUMPS FOR HEIGHT WITH MEDICINE BALL

**Coaching Points:** Initiate each jump with knees flexed at a 90° angle.
No pause between jumps.

## TWO LEGGED HOPPING OVER HURDLES

**Coaching Points:** Drive knees and arms aggressively up. Keep upper body vertical to keep from falling forward.

This drill can be done with 1, 2 or 3 hops between each low hurdle.

# Chapter V

**WHAT IS DEPTH JUMPING?**

Depth jumping, or box jumping, can be started after the athlete has gained sufficient strength to handle the additional stress. This technique involves jumping from a box to the ground followed immediately with another jump. The additional height of a box increases the force of gravity which causes a more forceful stretch of leg muscles. This adds to the concentric contraction when leaving the ground and it should result in a higher jump. The height of the boxes depends upon strength levels of the athletes. Highly trained Russian athletes have successfully used boxes 29"—42" high. For the average athlete, boxes 18"—24" high are recommended.

Research has shown that if the boxes are too high the concentric contraction is diminished due to an increased "lag" time between the eccentric stretch and the concentric contraction from the ground. Remember that the optimal concentric contraction occurs with the shortest possible lag time between the two contractions. Be aware that increasing the height of the boxes too quickly can increase the amount of stress on the joint areas and magnify the chance of injury.

Boxes can be made very inexpensively using strong plywood. We recommend that they be shaped in the form of a cut-off pyramid with a wide base for stability. Rubber strips should be glued to the top for traction. Gymnastic vault boxes with adjustable inserts can also be used for depth jumping.

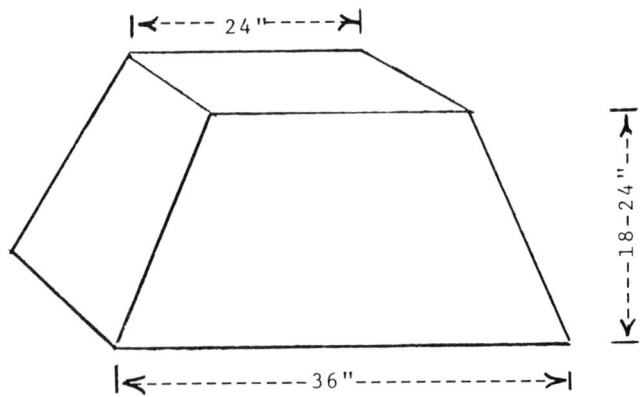

**RECOMMENDED DIMENSIONS FOR DEPTH JUMPING BOXES**

## DEPTH JUMPING DRILLS

**Two-Legged Jumps** *Onto* **Boxes**
   with 3 hops between boxes
   with 2 hops between boxes
   with 1 hop between boxes

**One-Legged Jumps** *Onto* **Boxes***
   with 3 hops between boxes
   with 2 hops between boxes
   with 1 hop between boxes

**Two-Legged Jumps** *Over* **Boxes**
   with 3 hops between boxes
   with 2 hops between boxes
   with 1 hop between boxes

   Alternate hops *onto* boxes with one hop between boxes (left-left, right-right)

   Repetitive side hops onto one box

   Rebound jumps off box (basketball rim or football goalpost crossbar needed)

   Distance between boxes can be adjusted according to needs.

*When performing a one-legged exercise always repeat the exercise with the opposite leg.

# Depth Jumping Drills

## Picture Descriptions

## TWO LEGGED JUMPS ONTO BOXES

**Coaching Points:** Attempt to land on ground with knees flexed. No pause between jumps. Drive arms aggressively up.

## ONE LEGGED JUMPS ONTO BOXES

**Coaching Points:** Lower boxes recommended for this drill.

## TWO LEGGED JUMPS OVER BOXES

**Coaching Points:** Emphasize forward, powerful action.
This drill can be done with 1, 2 or 3 hops between each box.

## ALTERNATE HOPS ONTO BOXES

**Coaching Points:** Good triple jump drill.
Sequence is Left-Left, Right-Right, Left-Left, Right-Right

## REPETITIVE SIDE HOPS ONTO BOX

**Coaching Points:** Very good drill for developing jumping ability. This is a very good conditioner for connective tissue in ankle joint.

## REBOUND JUMPS OFF BOX

**Coaching Points:** Jump high and hard off box and try to land with knees flexed.
Use basketball rim or crossbar of football goal post. Develops rebounding ability for basketball players.

# Chapter VI

### Plyometric Throwing Drills

This section includes drills that use a medicine ball or a throwing implement to strengthen the muscles used in the throwing motion. All movements must be explosive in nature. Explanations of technique accompany the pictures of each drill.

**Medicine Ball Throws**
 overhead catch and throw
 side catch and throw
 shot put catch and throw
 chest catch and throw

**Throws From a Box**
 shot put action
 discus throw action

# Throwing Drills

## Picture Descriptions

## MEDICINE BALL OVERHEAD CATCH AND THROW

**Coaching Points:** It is very important that the ball be in contact with the athlete for as little time as possible. This is an excellent exercise for quarterbacks and baseball players. Very good developer for abdominal muscle group.

## MEDICINE BALL SIDE CATCH AND THROW

**Coaching Points:** Keep legs wide for a solid base of support. Very good for track & field throwers and baseball players.

## MEDICINE BALL SHOT PUT CATCH AND THROW

**Coaching Points:** Medicine ball should be in contact with athlete for as short a time period as possible

# MEDICINE BALL CHEST CATCH AND THROW

**Coaching Points:** Key is to have the ball in contact with the athlete for as little time as possible. Good basketball drill—develops passing.

## SHOT PUT FROM BOX

**Coaching Points:** Land with knees flexed.
Jump hard off box, upon landing *explosively* complete the throw.
The time on the ground upon landing should be as short as possible.

## DISCUS THROW FROM BOX

**Coaching Points:** Land with knees flexed.

# CHAPTER VII
# COACHING POINTS FOR HOPPING, BOUNDING, AND DEPTH JUMPING

1. Be sure athletes are properly warmed up before initiating plyometric routines.
2. Upon contact with the ground, the athlete must rebound *immediately* and *explosively* off the ground in returning to the jump phase.
3. Athletes should keep their backs straight and as vertical as possible during the performance of the exercises.
4. Encourage athletes to utilize their arms to *lift* and *block* in coordination with the leg movements. This results in greater body lift.
5. Between each set of drills, it is advisable to have a recovery jog or walk back to the starting point.
6. Plyometric training can lead to muscle soreness during the initial stages of the program. All athletes should spend ample time on flexibility work every day.
7. It is common for athletes to train through minor injuries. Pay special attention to these athletes and watch for athletes susceptible to knee and lower back injuries. These athletes may not be suitable candidates for plyometric training. Coaches can select specific drills to be avoided by these individuals.
8. Encourage athletes to devise their own exercises, but make sure they conform to the concepts of plyometric training.
9. Plyometrics are not only a physiologically sound training technique, but they are easily lended as a group activity for integrating the team. In track and field, groups of athletes in different events are separated from each other on the practice field. Plyometrics are an ideal activity to consolidate the team.
10. Plyometrics are fun. Clutch, Wilton, McGown, and Bryce (1983) reported that their subjects enjoyed doing the depth jumps. These drills provide a variation from the normal grind of routine training. We have successfully used music during team plyometric training.
11. Plyometric exercises have an additional advantage over many other types of training. When many athletic budgets are being reduced, coaches appreciate that plyometrics are an inexpensive training method. Most schools have suitable mats for indoors and smooth stretches of grass

for outdoor training. Construction of boxes is also a minimal expense.
12 Think of plyometric drills as a progression—start easy and gradually increase the intensity as the athletes adapt to the stresses. Always monitor your athletes for injuries.

# CHAPTER VIII
# SUGGESTED PLYOMETRIC ROUTINES

Early Pre-season (one-two weeks into training, two times per week)
high knee running
butt kick running
alternate 4 high knee, 4 butt kick
alternate majorette step
one legged easy hopping
high knee skipping, for height & distance
two legged hopping—knees straight, for height
two legged hopping—knees to chest, for height
two legged hopping—heels to butt, for height
one legged hopping—knees straight, for height
alternate bounding, for height & distance
two legged squat jumps, for height
fast feet running
lunge hops

Pre-season (two times per week, one-two repetitions of each set)
high knee running
butt kick running
alternate 4 high knee, 4 butt kick
alternate majorette step
one legged easy hopping
high knee skipping, for height & distance
two legged hopping—knees straight, for height
two legged hopping—knees straight, for distance
two legged hopping—knees to chest
two legged hopping—heels to butt
two legged hopping with a twist
one legged hopping—knees straight, for height
one legged hopping, for height & distance
alternate bounding—knees straight, for height
alternate bounding, for height & distance
two legged squat jumps, for height
alternate hop, step, hop, step, for height & distance
two legged hopping, for distance
repeat triple jumps, for height & distance
two legged star jumps, for height
one legged hopping, for speed
fast feet running
two legged jump spins

lunge hops
medicine ball squat jumps (5 sets of 7 repetitions)
Competitive Season (two times per week, one repetition of each set)
See routine for pre-season and add:
Depth Jumping
two legged hops
  with 3 hops between boxes
  with 2 hops between boxes
  with 1 hop beween boxes
one legged hops
  with 3 hops between boxes
  with 2 hops between boxes
  with 1 hop between boxes
two legged hops over boxes
alternate double hops, 1 hop between boxes
  (left-left, right-right etc.)
Hurdle jumping
  with 3 hops between hurdles
  with 2 hops between hurdles
  with 1 hop between hurdles

# REFERENCES

Berger, R., 1982. *Applied Exercise Physiology.* Lea and Febiger. Philadelphia.

Blattner, S. and Noble, L., 1979. "Relative Effects of Isokinetic and Plyometric Training on Vertical Jumping Performance." *Research Quarterly.* Vol. 50, no. 4. pp 583-588.

Bunn, Jo., 1972. *Scientific Principles of Coaching.* 2nd ed. Prentice-Hall. Englewood Cliffs, NJ.

Burke, E., 1980. "Toward an Understanding of Human Performance." *Readings in Exercise Physiology for the Coach and Athlete.* 2nd ed. Movement Publications, NY.

Clutch, D., Wilton, M., McGown, C., Bryce, G. R., 1983. "The Effect of Depth Jumps and Weight Training on Leg Strength and Vertical Jump." *Research Quarterly for Exercise and Sport.* Vol. 54, no. 1 pp 5-10.

Ecker, T., 1976. *Track and Field, Technique Through Dynamics.* TAF News Press. Los Altos, CA.

Fox, E., 1979. *Sports Physiology.* Saunders College Publishing. Philadelphia.

Fritzche, F., 1981. *Leg Power Exercises for Young Athletes in The Jumps.* Edited by J. Jarver. TAF News Press. Los Altos, CA. pp 19-22.

Gambetta, V., 1981. *Plyometric Training in TAC Track and Field Coaching Manual.* Leisure Press. pp 34-36.

Gardner, W. and Osburn, W., 1973. *Structure of the Human Body.* 2nd ed. W. B. Saunders Co. Philadelphia.

Guyton, Arthur., 1974. *The Function of the Human Body.* 4th ed. W. B. Saunders Co. Philadelphia.

Hay, J., 1978. *The Biomechanics of Sports Techniques.* 2nd ed. Prentice-Hall. Englewood Cliffs, NJ.

Hochmuth, G., 1974. "Biomechanik Sport Licher Bewugungen." As quoted in *Modern Athlete and Coach* 12:5. pp 7-10.

Jarver, J., 1981. *Specific Power in Jumping in The Jumps.* TAF News Press. Los Altos, CA. pp 23-26.

Johnson, C., 1981. *Bounding For All in The Jumps.* Edited by J. Jarver. TAF News Press. Los Altos, CA. pp 16-18.

Mann, R., 1981. "Plyometrics Progression to Meet the Athletes Needs." *Scholastic Coach* 51:51-52.

Miller, B. and Power, S., 1981. "Developing Power in Athletics through the Process of Depth Jumping." *Athletics Coach.* Vol. 15, no. Z. June, 81.

Polhemus, R., Osina, M., Burkhardt, E., Patterson, M., 1980. "The Effects of Plyometric Training With Ankle and Vest Weights on Conventional Weight Training Programs for Men." *Track and Field Quarterly Review.* Winter, 80. pp 59-60.

Shaver, L., 1981. *Essentials of Exercise Physiology.* Burgess Publishing Co. Minneapolis.

Steben, R. and Steben, A., 1981. "The Validity of the Stretch Shortening Cycle in Selected Jumping Events." *J. Sports Medicine and Physical Fitness.* 21, 81. pp 28-37.

Strong, M., 1981. "Plyometric Training Procedures." *Track Technique Annual 1981.* pp 51-53.

Verhoshanski, Y., 1968. "Perspectives in the Improvement of Speed-Strength Preparation of Jumpers." *Yessis Review of Soviet Physical Education and Sports.* 3, pp 28-34.

Verhoshanski, Y., 1969. "Are Depth Jumps Useful?" *Yessis Review of Soviet Physical Education and Sports.* 4, pp 75-78.

Verhoshanski, Y. and Semyonov, V., 1978. *Strength Training For Sprinters In Sprints And Relays.* Edited by J. Jarver. TAF News Press. Los Altos, CA. pp 69-74.

Wilt, F., 1975. "Plyometrics: What it is—How it works." *Athletic Journal.* 1976. pp 89-90.